W9-CDF-136

Poetry for Young People

Rudyard Kipling

Edited by Eileen Gillooly
Illustrated by Jim Sharpe

Sterling Publishing Company, Inc.
New York

For Jake, and with special thanks to Ben, Kate, and Sam
—Eileen Gillooly

For Andy and Susie and all the times we've had
—Jim Sharpe

Library of Congress Cataloging-in-Publication Data

Kipling, Rudyard, 1865–1936.
    [Poems. Selections]
    Rudyard Kipling / edited by Eileen Gillooly; illustrator, Jim Sharpe.
      p.   cm. – (Poetry for young people)
    Includes index.
    Summary: An illustrated collection of twenty-eight notable poems by Rudyard Kipling, with commentary and definitions of unfamiliar words. Includes an introduction about the poet's life and work.
    ISBN 0-8069-4484-6
    1. Children's poetry, English. [1.English, poetry.] I. Gillooly, Eileen. II. Sharpe, Jim, ill. III. Title.
IV. Series.
PR4852.G55 2000
821'.8–DC21   99–042988

5   7   9   10   8   6   4

Published by Sterling Publishing Co., Inc.
387 Park Avenue South, New York, N.Y. 10016
Text © 2000 by Eileen Gillooly
Illustrations © 2000 by Jim Sharpe
Photograph on page 4 courtesy of the University of Sussex Library
Distributed in Canada by Sterling Publishing
c/o Canadian Manda Group, One Atlantic Avenue, Suite 105
Toronto, Ontario, Canada M6K 3E7
Distributed in Great Britain and Europe by Chris Lloyd at Orca Book Servies,
Stanley House, Fleets Lane, Poole BH15 3AJ England
Distributed in Australia by Capricorn Link (Australia) Pty Ltd.
P.O. Box 704, Windsor, NSW 2756 Australia

Printed in China
All rights reserved

Sterling ISBN 0-8069-4484-6

CONTENTS

Introduction: "I have written the tale of our life" 4
Prelude to *Departmental Ditties*   9

In the Beginning
Verses from "The White Seal"   10
Verse from "How the Whale Got His Throat"   12
Verses from "The Elephant's Child"   14
Verses from "The Cat That Walked by Himself"   15
Verses from "How the Camel Got His Hump"   16
Verses from "How the Leopard Got His Spots"   18

Growing Up
The Thousandth Man   19
If   20
Prophets at Home   22

At Home and Abroad
Neighbours   23
The Houses   24
The Beginning of the Armadilloes   25
The Ballad of East and West   26
To Thomas Atkins   27
Mandalay   28
Thorkild's Song   30

Tales and Legends
Letting in the Jungle   3
Mowgli's Brothers   33
Road-Song of the *Bandar-Log*   34
Harp Song of the Dane Women   36
The Way through the Woods   38

Past and Future
Cities and Thrones and Powers   39
A Song in Storm   40
The Benefactors   42
Natural Theology   44
Recessional   46
The Appeal   47
Index   48

INTRODUCTION
"I HAVE WRITTEN THE TALE OF OUR LIFE"

Rudyard Kipling, famous as the author of *The Jungle Book* and *Kim*, was also the most popular English poet of the late nineteenth century. His verses—whether in single poems like "If" (pages 20–21), collections like *Departmental Ditties* or *Barrack-Room Ballads* (see pages 9 and 27), or sprinkled throughout his fiction (such as those from the *Just So Stories*, pages 12–18)—express a remarkable variety of feelings and ideas. His audience was extraordinarily large, drawn from dozens of countries around the world. Many people consider him the last English-language poet to have won the admiration and appreciation of so vast a following. And in 1907, he became the first English writer to win the Nobel Prize for literature.

According to T. S. Eliot—one of the finest poets of the next generation—Kipling's outstanding achievement is his "emphatic sound," which like "the words of an orator or preacher are music." He meant that Kipling's poems, when read aloud, could exert a power over the listener that went far beyond the meaning of the words themselves. "There is no line of my verse," Kipling once wrote, "which has not been mouthed till the tongue has made it smooth." To see what he's talking about, look at "The Way through the Woods" on page 38. Notice the eerie, almost hypnotic effect he gets by repeating the phrase "the road through the woods." This phrase, like the ghostly road itself, seems to fade from one line of the poem only to appear suddenly everywhere else you turn.

Kipling constantly experimented with the structure, rhythms, and rhymes of his poems. He believed that a poem required expert craftsmanship as well as inspiration. So he always carefully chose words with the right "weights, colours, perfumes, and attributes." He borrowed his meter (rhythm) not only from traditional verse forms, but from contemporary music-hall ballads as well, reshaping it as needed. For unlike many poets of his day, he was not searching for a unique way to express himself. Instead, Kipling wanted to write for the largest possible audience about the emotions and ideas that he thought were common to everyone—to tell "the tale of our life" in all its fullness. He believed that "Men and Things come round again, eternal as the seasons," despite differences in time and place, class and skin color. Sometimes he demonstrates this by creating a character whose appearance and manner of speech may seem exotic to the reader—such as the Burmese girl in "Mandalay" (pages 28–29)—but whose feelings are actually familiar and easily shared. At other times, he points out that daily life is full of small opportunities for quiet heroic action (see "The Thousandth Man" on page 19, and "If" on pages 20–21).

Kipling thought if events and details were expressed in just the right way, they would be meaningful to everyone. To achieve this, the poet must, Kipling declared, learn "to think in another man's skin," to sympathize so fully with that other man that the reader would be able to feel his delight and pain. This was no easy task, since men come in "all makes, each with his life-tale, grievance, idea, ideal, or warning." But Kipling's own poetic imagination was extraordinary. In the poems collected here, you'll see how his quick, sympathetic, and often humorous perception gives us a sense of what it's like to be a British soldier, a child at sea, an ancient Dane woman, or even a baby seal or a jungle animal.

Rudyard Kipling, called "Ruddy" by his parents, was born on December 30, 1865, in Bombay, India. For many years, his father was the curator of the museum in the city of Lahore (now in Pakistan). Like many British children in India at this time, Kipling and his sister were sent to England to escape the dangerous illnesses that were then often fatal to the young in India. From the age of six until he was eleven years old, Kipling lived in the home of a paid caretaker who, together with her son, seems to have beaten and bullied him for most of those years. Kipling later traced his lifelong spells of insomnia to this harrowing time, as well as to his keen sympathy for the personal suffering of others. It "drained me of any capacity for real, personal hate for the rest of my days," he wrote in his autobiography, *Something of Myself*.

These bleak, soul-scarring years in the "House of Desolation," as he came to call it, were brightened only by his month-long Christmas visits to the London home of his uncle, the famous artist Edward Burne-Jones. The house was filled with the aroma of paint and the sound of stories told aloud. There Kipling contributed to the family magazine—"The Scribbler"—along with his cousins and the ever-present children of William Morris, another important artist. Morris was Kipling's honorary uncle (he called him "our Deputy Uncle Topsy").

Kipling read as much as he could whenever he could. When he was a boy, Emerson, Browning, Tennyson, and Poe were some of his favorite poets. Later in life, he concluded that perhaps the greatest lessons his parents had taught him were "that books and pictures were among the most important affairs in the world" and "that one could take pen and set down what one thought, and that nobody accused one of 'showing off' by doing so."

Kipling was eventually rescued from the House of Desolation by his mother and spent many months recuperating under her care. He was then sent to study at the United Services College, in a town with the odd name of Westward Ho! in Devonshire, England. (His novel *Stalky & Co.* recounts his adventures there.) Like most of his schoolmates, whose families also lived in British colonies, Kipling returned to India and, at the age of 16, began his professional life as a newspaperman. Because he worked long, long hours in the midst of often unbearable and disease-ridden heat, he referred to this period of his life as the "Seven Years' Hard," drawing a comparison with the grueling labor of prison life at the time. But his journalistic experience not only gave him the opportunity to publish his verses widely (*Departmental Ditties* first appeared in a newspaper), it also taught him how to be succinct (clear and concise), accurate in detail, and interested in the stories of other people. He believed these three qualities were responsible for his success as a writer.

He moved to London in 1889, and three years later married Caroline ("Carrie") Balestier, an American and the sister of a close friend. They took off on a honeymoon trip around the world, but financial problems forced them to stop when they reached Japan. The Kiplings hastily set sail for the United States and settled in Vermont, on property owned by Carrie's family. Here Kipling wrote *The Jungle Book* and *The Second Jungle Book*, perhaps his best-known works (you'll find four verses from these volumes on pages 10–11 and 32–35).

After four years, he and Carrie returned to England, eventually settling in Sussex in the village of Burwash. There, Kipling's interest in the prehistoric days of the region inspired two collections of fiction and several verses, including "Thorkild's Song" and "Harp Song of the Dane Women" (pages 30–31 and 36–37). Although the Kiplings made frequent trips to other parts of Europe throughout their lives, most often to France, and for a time spent six months of every year in South Africa, their house in Sussex was the place they called home until their deaths. Kipling kept a record of the many visitors to the house, which they called "Bateman's" (perhaps after a previous owner). The record noted the arrivals and departures of dear friends as well as complete strangers—and Kipling often marked his entries with private symbols. According to his daughter Elsie, the initials "F.I.P." stood for "fell in pond," which an astonishing number of his guests appear to have done. "Bateman's" is still open to visitors every year from April through October.

Despite his friendship with President Teddy Roosevelt, with whom he corresponded faithfully, Kipling never much liked the United States. His eldest child, Josephine, had died from pneumonia there when she was only six years old, and this memory made even the thought of another visit almost unbearable to him. Kipling also blamed the United States for its self-congratulation and lack of humility. His poem "Cities and Thrones and Powers" (page 39) has the U.S. at least partly in mind. Having treated its own native peoples so unfairly, it had no business, he felt, telling other nations how to treat theirs.

The hypocrisy of British "anti-Imperialists" who exploited the poor at home, while accusing their government of oppressing the people of India, made him angry, too. Kipling called himself an "Imperialist," by which he meant something less unpleasant than the word today generally means. He believed that the achievements of Britain—particularly its laws and social codes—should be exported throughout the world for the benefit of the rest of humanity. This is the Kipling of "Gunga Din" and "White Man's Burden"—two of his most famous poems, which, despite their fame and their author's good intentions, are hard for us to listen to today and are not included in this book. Even so, Kipling understood enough about India to know that the British presence there was not all good, and he often writes with more sympathy for the Indians than for their British rulers.

From about 1900 onward, many people objected to what they considered Kipling's extreme nationalism or sense of British superiority. They especially disapproved of his using poetry to promote his political views, which he felt a very real responsibility to do. As a result, in many of his later poems (see "Past and Future," pages 39–46), he sounds like a lone prophet preaching to a deaf audience. Yet "Prophets at Home" (page 22) is both intensely personal and historical, and exactly the sort of poem that Kipling most valued. In the same way, "A Song in Storm" (pages 40–41), written to commemorate those who fought on the British side in World War I, honors the selfless behavior of these individuals and their personal sacrifice. No one knew this sorrowful lesson better than Kipling, whose only son, John, died just weeks after arriving in France to fight. Barely 18 years old, he was reported missing in action at the Battle of Loos in Belgium in 1915 and declared dead more than two years later. His body was never found.

The deaths of Josephine and John haunted Kipling for the rest of his life. His one unfailing consolation was the close companionship of Elsie, his only remaining child, who lived with her parents until her marriage in 1924. Soon after his son's death, however, Kipling's health broke down, and for more than fifteen years he suffered from an undiagnosed ulcer, which eventually proved fatal. He died on January 18, 1936, his and Carrie's forty-fourth wedding anniversary and just two days before the death of his good friend, King George V of England. Both are buried in Westminster Abbey. Kipling's grave lies in Poets' Corner, near those of Charles Dickens and Thomas Hardy, two other great English writers of the nineteenth century. His funeral service ended with the singing of his own already famous poem "Recessional," verses from which can be found on page 46.

PRELUDE TO *DEPARTMENTAL DITTIES*

These verses begin Kipling's first collection of poetry, Departmental Ditties, *published when he was just 20 years old. Although a ditty is a simple, lighthearted verse form that often makes fun of its subject, Kipling here assures the British government officials in India—the subject of his ditties—of his sympathy for their cares, their "toil" and "woe." Kipling hoped not only to share their experience with readers in England, but to get them to laugh at themselves as well.*

I have eaten your bread and salt.
   I have drunk your water and wine.
The deaths ye died I have watched beside,
   And the lives ye led were mine.

Was there aught that I did not share
   In vigil or toil or ease,—
One joy or woe that I did not know,
   Dear hearts across the seas?

I have written the tale of our life
   For a sheltered people's mirth,
In jesting guise—but ye are wise,
   And ye know what the jest is worth.

ye—*you*
aught—*anything*
vigil—*watchful attention*
toil—*labor*
woe—*sorrow*
mirth—*laughing amusement*
guise—*appearance*
jesting—*joking*

VERSES FROM "THE WHITE SEAL"

A mother seal sings a lullaby to her baby in this verse from a chapter of The Jungle Book. *The rhythms of the poem, like the waves they describe, soothingly rock the baby to sleep, while the mother's words reassure her baby of her loving protection.*

Oh! hush thee, my baby, the night is behind us,
    And black are the waters that sparkled so green.
The moon, o'er the combers, looks downward to find us
    At rest in the hollows that rustle between.
Where billow meets billow, there soft be thy pillow;
    Ah, weary wee flipperling, curl at thy ease!
The storm shall not wake thee, nor shark overtake thee,
    Asleep in the arms of the slow-swinging seas.

o'er—*over*
combers—*long curling waves*
billow—*great surge of water*
flipperling—*baby seal*

10

VERSE FROM "HOW THE WHALE GOT HIS THROAT"

The grown-ups on board a ship in the stormy North Atlantic are seasick. But the young child here is only a little bewildered—and more delighted—by all the excitement. This verse and those through page 18 come from the Just So Stories.

When the cabin port-holes are dark and green
   Because of the seas outside;
When the ship goes *wop* (with a wiggle between)
And the steward falls into the soup-tureen,
   And the trunks begin to slide;
When Nursey lies on the floor in a heap,
And Mummy tells you to let her sleep,
And you aren't waked or washed or dressed,
Why, then you will know (if you haven't guessed)
You're "Fifty North and Forty West!"

steward—*ship's officer in charge of dining*
   arrangements
tureen—*a deep, broad dish*
Fifty North and Forty West—*in the middle*
   of the Atlantic Ocean

13

VERSES FROM "THE ELEPHANT'S CHILD"

Kipling wrote this poem to celebrate his young daughter Elsie—
whom he nicknamed "Elsie Why"—and her ceaseless questions.

I keep six honest serving-men
   (They taught me all I knew);
Their names are What and Why and When
   And How and Where and Who.
I send them over land and sea,
   I send them east and west;
But after they have worked for me,
   I give them all a rest.

I let them rest from nine till five,
   For I am busy then,
As well as breakfast, lunch and tea,
   For they are hungry men.
But different folk have different views.
   I know a person small—
She keeps ten million serving-men,
   Who get no rest at all!

She sends 'em abroad on her own affairs,
   From the second she opens her eyes—
One million Hows, two million Wheres,
   And seven million Whys!

VERSES FROM "THE CAT THAT WALKED BY HIMSELF"

Cats are famous for their independence, which the child speaking in this poem both admires and regrets. Dogs, on the other hand, are as a rule utterly faithful and wonderfully appreciative—trusty companions ever since cave-dwelling days.

Pussy can sit by the fire and sing,
   Pussy can climb a tree,
Or play with a silly old cork and string
   To 'muse herself, not me.
But *I* like *Binkie* my dog, because
   He knows how to behave;
So, *Binkie's* the same as the First Friend was,
   And I am the Man in the Cave!

Pussy will play Man Friday till
   It's time to wet her paw
And make her walk on the window-sill
   (For the footprint Crusoe saw);
Then she fluffles her tail and mews,
   And scratches and won't attend.
But *Binkie* will play whatever I choose,
   And he is my true First Friend!

Pussy will rub my knees with her head
   Pretending she loves me hard;
But the very minute I go to my bed
   Pussy runs out in the yard,
And there she stays till the morning-light;
   So I know it is only pretend;
But *Binkie*, he snores at my feet all night,
   And he is my Firstest Friend!

Man Friday—*Robinson Crusoe's trustworthy companion in Defoe's famous novel*
Crusoe—*the hero of* Robinson Crusoe, *by Daniel Defoe*
fluffles—*puffs out in a fluffy mass*
attend—*pay attention*

VERSES FROM "HOW THE CAMEL GOT HIS HUMP"

Grumpiness is something everyone suffers at times—"kiddies and grown-ups too." Here Kipling suggests working in the garden as a way to get the best of a bad mood. Even more importantly, he shows how joking about grouchiness helps make it disappear.

The Camel's hump is an ugly lump
   Which well you may see at the Zoo;
But uglier yet is the hump we get
   From having too little to do.

Kiddies and grown-ups too-oo-oo,
If we haven't enough to do-oo-oo,
          We get the hump—
          Cameelious hump—
The hump that is black and blue!

We climb out of bed with a frouzly head,
   And a snarly-yarly voice.
We shiver and scowl and we grunt and we growl
   At our bath and our boots and our toys;

And there ought to be a corner for me
(And I know there is one for you)
          When we get the hump—
          Cameelious hump—
The hump that is black and blue!

The cure for this ill is not to sit still,
   Or frowst with a book by the fire;
But to take a large hoe and a shovel also,
   And dig till you gently perspire;

And then you will find that the sun and the wind,
And the Djinn of the Garden too,
          Have lifted the hump—
          The horrible hump—
The hump that is black and blue!

I get it as well as you-oo-oo—
If I haven't enough to do-oo-oo!
We all get hump—
Cameelious hump—
Kiddies and grown-ups too!

frouzly—*untidy, rumpled-haired*
frowst—*rest lazily*
Djinn—*spirit*
snarly-yarly—*growling*
Cameelious—*very camel-like*

VERSES FROM
"HOW THE LEOPARD GOT HIS SPOTS"

Escaping from everyday routine—especially with one's father as a companion—can be a very special pleasure. Kipling uses the verse form known as a dramatic monologue to convey a sense of the child's personality as he coaxes his father to play. In a dramatic monologue, the speaker talks to other characters in the poem, but we never hear their responses directly. We only know of their presence from what the speaker says.

I am the Most Wise Baviann, saying in most wise tones,
"Let us melt into the landscape—just us two by our lones."
People have come—in a carriage-calling. But Mummy is there. . . .
Yes, I can go if you take me—Nurse says *she* don't care.
Let's go up to the pig-styes and sit on the farmyard rails!
Let's say things to the bunnies, and watch 'em skitter their tails.
Let's—oh, *anything*, daddy, so long as it's you and me,
And going truly exploring, and not being in till tea!
Here's your boots (I've brought 'em), and here's your cap and stick,
And here's your pipe and tobacco. Oh, come along out of it—quick!

Baviann—*Dutch for "baboon"*
lones—*selves*
skitter—*move rapidly*

THE THOUSANDTH MAN

Great friendship of the sort described in this first stanza of "The Thou-sandth Man" is a rare and precious thing. The speaker's language identi-fies him as a common man, as does his advice, which is simple and direct.

One man in a thousand, Solomon says,
Will stick more close than a brother.
And it's worth while seeking him half your days
If you find him before the other.
Nine hundred and ninety-nine depend
On what the world sees in you,
But the Thousandth Man will stand your friend
With the whole round world agin you.

Solomon—*biblical king, famous for his wisdom*   agin—*against*

If

Even in his lifetime, "If" was one of the most popular of Kipling's poems. Teachers would often make their students copy its verses as punishment for misbehaving, "which did me no good with the Young when I met them later," Kipling complained. Notice that the entire poem is actually one very long sentence.

If you can keep your head when all about you
    Are losing theirs and blaming it on you,
If you can trust yourself when all men doubt you,
    But make allowance for their doubting too;
If you can wait and not be tired by waiting,
    Or being lied about, don't deal in lies,
Or being hated, don't give way to hating,
    And yet don't look too good, nor talk too wise:

If you can dream—and not make dreams your master;
    If you can think—and not make thoughts your aim;
If you can meet with Triumph and Disaster
    And treat those two imposters just the same;
If you can bear to hear the truth you've spoken
    Twisted by knaves to make a trap for fools,
Or watch the things you gave your life to, broken,
    And stoop and build 'em up with worn-out tools:

If you can make one heap of all your winnings
    And risk it on one turn of pitch-and-toss,
And lose, and start again at your beginnings
    And never breathe a world about your loss;
If you can force your heart and nerve and sinew
    To serve your turn long after they are gone,
And so hold on when there is nothing in you
    Except the Will which says to them: "Hold on!"

If you can talk with crowds and keep your virtue,
    Or walk with Kings—nor lose the common touch,
If neither foes nor loving friends can hurt you,
    If all men count with you, but none too much;
If you can fill the unforgiving minute
    With sixty seconds' worth of distance run,
Yours is the Earth and everything that's in it,
    And—which is more—you'll be a Man, my son!

knaves—*dishonest,
    untrustworthy people*
pitch-and-toss—*coin
    game combining skill
    and chance*
sinew—*muscular
    power*
virtue—*moral goodness*

PROPHETS AT HOME

In the voice of a country villager, the speaker observes that no matter how important and famous you become, you're not likely to be treated as a celebrity by those who knew you as a child. Your home town, however, offers you what no other place can: simple acceptance rather than earned respect.

Prophets have honour all over the Earth,
    Except in the village where they were born,
Where such as knew them boys from birth
    Nature-ally hold 'em in scorn.

When Prophets are naughty and young and vain,
    They make a won'erful grievance of it;
(You can see by their writings how they complain),
    But O, 'tis won'erful good for the Prophet!

There's nothing Nineveh Town can give
    (Nor being swallowed by whales between),
Makes up for the place where a man's folk live,
    Which don't care nothing what he has been.
He might ha' been that, or he might ha' been this,
But they love and they hate him for what he is.

prophets—*predictors of the future, especially divinely inspired ones*
vain—*excessively proud*
grievance—*a wrong considered worthy of complaint*
Nineveh—*ancient Assyrian city on the Tigris River, where the prophet Jonah was*
    sent by God to preach

NEIGHBOURS

*To be a good neighbor—as to be a good friend—
requires thinking as much about the effects of your
actions upon others as upon yourself. The speaker in
this first stanza of Kipling's poem predicts a life full
of blessings for the worthy neighbor: health, luck,
happiness, true friends, and a loving wife.*

The man that is open of heart to his neighbour,
   And stops to consider his likes and dislikes,
His blood shall be wholesome whatever his labour,
   His luck shall be with him whatever he strikes.
The Splendour of Morning shall duly possess him,
   That he may not be sad at the falling of eve.
And, when he has done with mere living—God bless him!—
   A many shall sigh, and one Woman shall grieve!

splendour—*great light; glory*
duly—*at the proper time*
grieve—*mourn*

23

THE HOUSES

*No matter how widely we travel or how many friends we have,
the relationships we have with our neighbors greatly affect us
all. Here the speaker reminds us that our own happiness
depends upon the respect, care, and consideration we show to
those in the house—or the country—next door.*

’Twixt my house and thy house the pathway is broad,
In thy house or my house is half the world’s hoard;
By my house and thy house hangs all the world’s fate,
On thy house and my house lies half the world’s hate.

For my house and thy house no help shall we find
Save thy house and my house—kin cleaving to kind;
If my house be taken, thine tumbleth anon.
If thy house be forfeit, mine followeth soon.

’Twixt my house and thy house what talk can there be
Of headship or lordship, or service or fee?
Since my house to thy house no greater can send
Than thy house to my house—friend comforting friend;
And thy house to my house no meaner can bring
Than my house to thy house—King counselling King!

hoard—*hidden wealth*   tumbleth—*fall down*
kin—*relatives*   anon—*in a short time*
cleaving—*clinging*   forfeit—*surrendered*
thine—*yours*   headship—*leadership*

THE BEGINNING OF THE ARMADILLOES

The excitement of travel fills this most joyful of Kipling's poems. In these stanzas, notice how both the look of the poem spreads across the page and the frequent sound of "roll down" helps to create the feeling of high-spirited movement.

I've never sailed the Amazon,
    I've never reached Brazil;
But the *Don* and *Magdalena*,
    They can go there when they will!

        Yes, weekly from Southampton,
        Great steamers, white and gold,
        Go rolling down to Rio
        (Roll down—roll down to Rio!).
        And I'd like to roll to Rio
        Some day before I'm old!

I've never seen a Jaguar,
    Nor yet an Armadill-
o dilloing in his armour,
    And I s'pose I never will,

        Unless I go to Rio
        These wonders to behold—
        Roll down—roll down to Rio—
        Roll really down to Rio!
        Oh, I'd love to roll to Rio
        Some day before I'm old!

Don and *Magdalena*—*names of ships*
Southampton—*a major port city, on the south coast of England*
Rio—*Rio de Janeiro, city in Brazil*

THE BALLAD OF EAST AND WEST

This is the opening verse of the poem that made Kipling famous. It is odd that the first line of the poem is often quoted by itself, because the idea it expresses is contradicted by the third and fourth lines. This annoyed Kipling, who called the first line a "glittering generality."

Oh, East is East, and West is West, and never the twain shall meet,
Till Earth and Sky stand presently at God's great Judgment Seat;
But there is neither East nor West, Border, nor Breed, nor Birth,
When two strong men stand face to face, though they come from the ends of the earth!

twain—*set of two*
breed—*ethnic group*
birth—*class status*

TO THOMAS ATKINS

Kipling trusted the common British soldier more than the politicians and high-ranking officers who ordered him about. This prelude to Kipling's book Barrack-Room Ballads *is a tribute to the ordinary British military man—otherwise known as a "Tommy"—whose sacrifices for his country, Kipling felt, were seldom properly acknowledged or appreciated.*

I have made for you a song,
   And it may be right or wrong,
But only you can tell me if it's true.
   I have tried for to explain
   Both your pleasure and your pain,
And, Thomas, here's my best respects to you!

O there'll surely come a day
   When they'll give you all your pay,
And treat you as a Christian ought to do;
   So, until that day comes round,
   Heaven keep you safe and sound,
And, Thomas, here's my best respects to you!

MANDALAY

"Mandalay," the first stanza of which is reprinted here, became a popular favorite almost immediately upon its publication. In just a few words, Kipling conjures a scene rich in atmosphere and color about a British soldier's romance with the young Burmese woman he's left behind. The language of the poem is full of unusual sights and sounds mixed together—from temple bells and a thundering dawn to chunking paddles and the use of dialects.

By the old Moulmein Pagoda, lookin' lazy at the sea,
There's a Burma girl a-settin', and I know she thinks o' me;
For the wind is in the palm-trees, and the temple-bells they say:
"Come you back, you British soldier; come you back to Mandalay!"
   Come you back to Mandalay,
   Where the old Flotilla lay:
   Can't you 'ear their paddles chunkin' from Rangoon to Mandalay?
   On the road to Mandalay,
   Where the flyin'-fishes play,
   An' the dawn comes up like thunder outer China 'crost the Bay!

Rangoon—*capital of Burma*
Mandalay—*city in Burma*
Moulmein—*city in Burma*
pagoda—*a temple in the Far East*
flotilla—*a group of naval vessels*
chunkin'—*making a dull, throbbing sound*
'crost—*across*

THORKILD'S SONG

More than 1,000 years ago, Vikings from Scandinavia, crossing the rough seas of the North Atlantic in large ships, attacked England on various occasions, raiding its coastline and penetrating inland where they could. Kipling was fascinated by the ancient history of Sussex, where he resided for many years, and by the archaeological evidence he found there of these unwelcome visitors. This poem mimics the rhythms of a rowing song. Kipling imagines the Vikings' longing to reach home as the fuel that drives their return.

There's no wind along these seas,
Out oars for Stavenger!
Forward all for Stavenger!
So we must wake the white-ash breeze,
Let fall for Stavenger!
A long pull for Stavenger!

Oh, hear the benches creak and strain!
(A long pull for Stavenger!)
She thinks she smells the Northland rain!
(A long pull for Stavenger!)

She thinks she smells the Northland snow,
And she's as glad as we to go.

She thinks she smells the Northland rime,
And the dear dark nights of winter-time.

She wants to be at her own home pier,
To shift her sails and standing gear.

She wants to be in her winter-shed,
To strip herself and go to bed.

Her very bolts are sick for shore,
And we—we want it ten times more!

So all you Gods that love brave men,
Send us a three-reef gale again!

Send us a gale, and watch us come,
With close-cropped canvas slashing home!

But—there's no wind on all these seas,
A long pull for Stavenger!
So we must wake the white-ash breeze,
A long pull for Stavenger!

Stavenger—*Stavanger, a seaport in Norway*
standing gear—*objects fixed in place on*
   a ship, moved only for repairs
gale—*a very strong wind*
close-cropped—*cut short*
canvas—*material from which sails are made*
white-ash breeze—*ocean spray caused both by*
   rowing and by mortal spirit

LETTING IN THE JUNGLE

Throughout India, even today, there are ruins of abandoned cities, where the jungle has all but reclaimed the territory once occupied by people. This stanza from "Letting in the Jungle" calls attention to the fact that, to the animals who live there, such an event is a cause for rejoicing.

Veil them, cover them, wall them round—
    Blossom, and creeper, and weed—
Let us forget the sight and the sound,
    The smell and the touch of the breed!
Fat black ash by the altar-stone,
    Here is the white-foot rain,
And the does bring forth in the fields unsown,
    And none shall affright them again;
And the blind walls crumble, unknown, o'erthrown,
    And none shall inhabit again!

breed—*type of domesticated*
    animal; here, mankind
unsown—*not cultivated*

MOWGLI'S BROTHERS

If in civilization, human laws of order and property and obedience govern, in the jungle— at night at least —wild-ness reigns, and it's every beast for itself. The stanza below, from "Mowgli's Brothers," reveals this law of the jungle.

Now Chil the Kite brings home the night
That Mang the Bat sets free—
The herds are shut in byre and hut,
For loosed till dawn are we.
This is the hour of pride and power,
Talon and tush and claw.
Oh, hear the call!— Good hunting all
That keep the Jungle Law!

kite	*hawk*	talon	*claw of a bird of prey*
byre	*cow shed*	tush	*tusk*

ROAD-SONG OF THE *BANDAR-LOG*

In The Jungle Book, *where these verses first appeared, the Bandar-Log—the Hindi word for "Monkey People"— are shunned by their fellow jungle creatures because they show no respect for others and never accomplish any- thing. They greatly enjoy playing pranks and teasing, however (here they are teasing other animals for having droopy tails).*

Here we go in a flung festoon,
Half-way up to the jealous moon!
Don't you envy our pranceful bands?
Don't you wish you had extra hands?
Wouldn't you like if your tails were—*so*—
Curved in the shape of a Cupid's bow?
   Now you're angry, but—never mind,
   Brother, thy tail hangs down behind!

Here we sit in a branchy row,
Thinking of beautiful things we know;
Dreaming of deeds that we mean to do,
All complete, in a minute or two—
Something noble and grand and good,
Won by merely wishing we could.
   Now we're going to—never mind,
   Brother, thy tail hangs down behind!

All the talk we ever have heard
Uttered by bat or beast or bird—
Hide or fin or scale or feather—
Jabber it quickly and all together!
Excellent! Wonderful! Once again!
Now we are talking just like men.
   Let's pretend we are . . . Never mind!
   Brother, thy tail hangs down behind!
   This is the way of the Monkey-kind!

flung—*thrown with energy and abandon*
festoon—*a garland suspended in a curve between two points*
pranceful—*lively, strutting; moving by springs and bounds*
Cupid's bow—*the semi- circular hunting bow carried by the infant Roman god of love*
jabber—*say rapidly and un- intelligibly; babble*

HARP SONG OF THE DANE WOMEN

Ever since ancient times, men have gone off to war, leaving women to grieve their absence. This poem should be read with "Thorkild's Song" in mind (pages 30–31), since it tells the story of the Viking attacks on England long ago from the point of view of the Viking (or Dane) women. In their lament, the women blame the ocean for stealing their sailor-husbands away.

What is a woman that you forsake her,
And the hearth-fire and the home-acre,
To go with the old grey Widow-maker?

She has no house to lay a guest in—
But one chill bed for all to rest in,
That the pale suns and the stray bergs nest in.

She has no strong white arms to fold you,
But the ten-times-fingering weed to hold you—
Out on the rocks where the tide has rolled you.

Yet, when the signs of summer thicken,
and the ice breaks, and the birch-buds quicken,
Yearly you turn from our side, and sicken—

Sicken again for the shouts and the slaughters.
You steal away to the lapping waters,
And look at your ship in her winter-quarters.

You forget our mirth, and talk at the tables,
The kine in the shed and the horse in the stables—
To pitch her sides and go over her cables.

Then you drive out where the storm-clouds swallow,
And the sound of your oar-blades, falling hollow,
Is all we have left through the months to follow.

Ah, what is Woman that you forsake her,
And the hearth-fire and the home-acre,
To go with the old grey Widow-maker?

old grey Widow-maker—*ocean*
forsake—*leave altogether; abandon*
hearth-fire—*fireplace; symbol of home*
bergs—*icebergs*
quicken—*come to life*
mirth—*laughter*
kine—*cattle*
pitch—*smear with a waterproofing substance*

THE WAY THROUGH THE WOODS

Past twilight the world has a different look, especially in the woods, when the wildlife awakens. It seems appropriate that this slightly spooky verse comes from a chapter called "Marklake Witches," in a book entitled Rewards and Fairies.

They shut the road through the woods
Seventy years ago.
Weather and rain have undone it again,
And now you would never know
There was once a road through the woods
Before they planted the trees.
It is underneath the coppice and heath
And the thin anemones.
Only the keeper sees
That, where the ring-dove broods,
And the badgers roll at ease,
There was once a road through the woods.

Yet, if you enter the woods
Of a summer evening late,
When the night-air cools on the trout-ringed pools
Where the otter whistles his mate,
(They fear not men in the woods,
Because they see so few.)
You will hear the beat of a horse's feet,
And the swish of a skirt in the dew,
Steadily cantering through
The misty solitudes,
As though they perfectly knew
The old lost road through the woods. . . .
But there is no road through the woods.

coppice—*thicket; dense growth of shrubs*
heath—*uncultivated land covered with low-growing shrubs*
anenomes—*a type of flower*
ring-dove—*wood pigeon*
broods—*sits on eggs to hatch them*
cantering—*faster than trotting, but slower than galloping*

CITIES AND THRONES AND POWERS

"Every nation, like every individual, walks in a vain show," thinking itself more important than others, "else it could not live with itself," Kipling once wrote. The speaker here, however, points out that in the vastness of time mighty nations and fragile daffodils are both short-lived.

Cities and Thrones and Powers
   Stand in Time's eye,
Almost as long as flowers,
   Which daily die:
But, as new buds put forth
   To glad new men,
Out of the spent and unconsidered Earth
   The Cities rise again.

This season's Daffodil,
   She never hears
What change, what chance, what chill,
   Cut down last year's;
But with bold countenance,
   And knowledge small,
Esteems her seven days' continuance
   To be perpetual.

So Time that is o'er-kind
   To all that be,
Ordains us e'en as blind,
   As bold as she:
That in our very death,
   And burial sure,
Shadow to shadow, well persuaded, saith,
   "See how our works endure!"

spent—*used up*
unconsidered—*unthinking*
countenance—*appearance; look on one's face*
continuance—*continuation*
esteems—*respectfully regards*
perpetual—*lasting forever*
ordains—*decrees*
endure—*continue to exist*

A Song in Storm
1914–18

Kipling here compares World War I to a storm at sea, in which having right on one's side is meaningless in the face of overwhelming force. The speaker advises humility before the unknown and respect for the power of the enemy—whether that enemy be the German military or the stormy seas themselves. Although the poem celebrates the courage of the sailors and their willingness to sacrifice themselves for the good of the whole, we still hear (buried in the "etc.") a cry of sympathy for their individual suffering.

Be well assured that on our side
  The abiding oceans fight,
Though headlong wind and heaping tide
  Make us their sport to-night.
By force of weather, not of war,
  In jeopardy we steer:
Then welcome Fate's discourtesy
  Whereby it shall appear
    How in all time of our distress,
    And our deliverance too,
    The game is more than the player of the game,
    And the ship is more than the crew!

Out of the mist into the mirk
  The glimmering combers roll.
Almost these mindless waters work
  As though they had a soul—
Almost as though they leagued to whelm
  Our flag beneath their green:
Then welcome Fate's discourtesy
  Whereby it shall be seen, etc.

Be well assured, though wave and wind
  Have mightier blows in store,
That we who keep the watch assigned
  Must stand to it the more;
And as our streaming bows rebuke
  Each billow's baulked career,
Sing, welcome Fate's discourtesy
  Whereby it is made clear, etc.

No matter though our decks be swept
  And mast and timber crack—

We can make good all loss except
  The loss of turning back.
So, 'twixt these Devils and our deep
  Let courteous trumpets sound,
To welcome Fate's discourtesy
  Whereby it will be found, etc.

Be well assured, though in our power
  Is nothing left to give
But chance and place to meet the hour,
  And leave to strive to live,
Till these dissolve our Order holds,
  Our Service binds us here.
Then welcome Fate's discourtesy
  Whereby it is made clear
    How in all time of our distress,
    As in our triumph too,
    The game is more than the player of the game,
    And the ship is more than the crew!

abiding—*continuing always*
jeopardy—*danger of severe injury*
combers—*waves*
leagued—*worked together*
whelm—*cover with water*
rebuke—*check; stop from proceeding*
billow—*great surge of water*
baulked—*thwarted; stopped from proceeding*

THE BENEFACTORS

Sometimes a casual tone and an ironic perspective can make a serious point. "The Benefactors" playfully looks at human progress in developing weapons of war—from tooth and nail to guns by the millions. In the stanzas reprinted here, the poet asks us to consider how beneficial or progressive such so-called progress actually is.

It is not learning, grace nor gear,
　　Nor easy meat and drink,
But bitter pinch of pain and fear
　　That makes creation think.

When in this world's unpleasing youth
　　Our godlike race began,
The longest arm, the sharpest tooth,
　　Gave man control of man;

Till, bruised and bitten to the bone
　　And taught by pain and fear,
He learned to deal the far-off stone,
　　and poke the long, safe spear.

So tooth and nail were obsolete
　　As means against a foe,
Till, bored by uniform defeat,
　　Some genius built the bow.

Then stone and javelin proved as vain
　　As old-time tooth and nail;
Till, spurred anew by fear and pain,
　　Man fashioned coats of mail.

Then was there safety for the rich
　　And danger for the poor,
Till someone mixed a power which
　　Redressed the scale once more.

Helmut and armour disappeared
　　With sword and bow and pike,
And, when the smoke of battle cleared,
　　All men were armed alike. . . .

And when ten million such were slain
　　To please one crazy king,
Man, schooled in bulk by fear and pain,
　　Grew weary of the thing;

And, at the very hour designed
　　To enslave him past recall,
His tooth-stone-arrow-gun-shy mind
　　Turned and abolished all.

All Power, each Tyrant, every Mob
　　Whose head has grown too large,
Ends by destroying its own job
　　And works its own discharge.

obsolete—*out of date, no longer useful*
foe—*enemy*
uniform—*unvarying*
coats of mail—*armor made from small loops of chain*
redressed—*adjusted to make even*
schooled—*taught, trained*
bulk—*great portion*
recall—*changing or taking back an order*
discharge—*firing of a weapon*

NATURAL THEOLOGY

Humor and history again join forces to teach a lesson—this time, to demonstrate that even though we can't know beforehand the consequences of our actions, we must still take responsibility for the choices we make. Here, in a few stanzas, Kipling shows how believers of various sorts—primitive, pagan, and Christian—blame God for the suffering they've brought on themselves.

PRIMITIVE

I ate my fill of a whale that died
    And stranded after a month at sea. . . .
There is a pain in my inside.
    Why have the Gods afflicted me?
Ow! I am purged till I am a wraith!
    Wow! I am sick till I cannot see!
What is the sense of Religion and Faith?
    Look how the Gods have afflicted me!

PAGAN

How can the skin of rat or mouse hold
    Anything more than a harmless flea? . . .
The burning plague has taken my household.
    Why have my Gods afflicted me?
All my kith and kin are deceased,
    Though they were as good as good could be.
I will out and batter the family priest,
    Because my Gods have afflicted me!

MEDIÆVAL

My privy and well drain into each other
    After the custom of Christendie. . . .
Fevers and fluxes are wasting my mother.
    Why has the Lord afflicted me?
The Saints are helpless for all I offer—
    So are the clergy I used to fee.
Henceforward I keep my cash in my coffer,
    Because the Lord has afflicted me.

CHORUS

We had a kettle: we let it leak:
    Our not repairing it made it worse.
We haven't had any tea for a week. . . .
    The bottom is out of the Universe!

CONCLUSION

This was none of the good Lord's pleasure,
    For the Spirit He breathed in Man is free;
But what comes after is measure for measure
    And not a God that afflicteth thee.
As was the sowing so the reaping
    Is now and evermore shall be.
Thou art delivered to thine own keeping.
    Only Thyself hath afflicted thee!

afflicted—*caused to suffer*
purged—*emptied of food and waste*
wraith—*ghost*
kith and kin—*friends and relatives*
batter—*beat, hit*
privy—*outhouse, latrine*
Christendie—*the Christian world; that is, Europe 1,000*
    years ago
fluxes—*fluid discharge from the body*
to fee—*to give a tip to*
coffer—*strongbox for storing money*

RECESSIONAL

Urged to write a poem to commemorate the 70th year of Queen Victoria's reign, Kipling instead wrote this "hymn." It warns England against being smug and arrogant in its role as a world-leading nation. England was then at war in South Africa against the Boers (Dutch settlers). "At the back of my head there was an uneasiness," Kipling tells us in his autobiography, and the national "optimism . . . scared me. The outcome . . . took the shape of a set of verses called 'Recessional.'" The first, second and fifth stanzas are reprinted here. Although the speaker hints at his audience's lost faith, the poem—or hymn— prays for guidance, protection, and mercy.

God of our fathers, known of old,
   Lord of our far-flung battle-line,
Beneath whose awful Hand we hold
   Dominion over palm and pine—
Lord God of Hosts, be with us yet,
Lest we forget—lest we forget!

The tumult and the shouting dies;
   The Captains and the Kings depart:
Still stands Thine ancient sacrifice,
   An humble and a contrite heart.
Lord God of Hosts, be with us yet,
Lest we forget—lest we forget!

For heathen heart that puts her trust
   In reeking tube and iron shard,
All valiant dust that builds on dust,
   And guarding, calls not Thee to guard,
For frantic boast and foolish word—
Thy mercy on Thy People, Lord!

recessional—*a hymn sung as clergy and
   choir exit a church after services*
awful—*inspiring awe*
dominion—*control*
lest—*unless*
tumult—*riot, din and commotion*
contrite—*repentant, sorry*
heathen—*one who believes in other than
   the God of Judaism, Christianity, or Islam*

reeking tube—*smoking rifle*
shard—*fragment of metal; here, bullet*
valiant—*courageous*

THE APPEAL

If I have given you delight
    By aught that I have done,
Let me lie quiet in that night
    Which shall be yours anon:

And for the little, little, span
    The dead are borne in mind,
Seek not to question other than
    The books I leave behind.

aught—*anything*
anon—*soon*
span—*period of time*
borne—*carried*

INDEX

Atkins, Thomas, 27
Atlantic Ocean, 12
Balestier, Caroline ("Carrie"), 6
Ballad of East and West, The, 26
Bandar-Log, 34
Barrack-Room Ballads, 4, 27
Bateman's, 7
Battle of Loos, 7
Beginning of the Armadilloes, The, 25
Benefactors, The, 42
Boer War, 46
Bombay, India, 5
Browning, Robert, 6
Burne-Jones, Edward, 6
Burwash, Sussex, England, 6
Cat That Walked by Himself, The, 15
Cities and Thrones and Powers, 6, 39
Departmental Ditties, 4, 6, 9
Dickens, Charles, 8
Elephant's Child, The, 14
Eliot, T.S., 4
Emerson, Ralph Waldo, 6
George V, 8
Grouchiness, 16–17
Gunga Din, 7
Hardy, Thomas, 8
Harp Song of the Dane Women, 6, 36–37
House of Desolation, 5–6

Houses, The, 24
How the Camel Got His Hump, 16–17
How the Leopard Got His Spots, 18
How the Whale Got His Throat, 12–13
Hymn, 46
If, 4, 5, 20–21
Imperialist, 7
Jungle Book, 4, 6, 10, 34
Just So Stories, 4, 12–18
Kim, 4
Kipling, Elsie, 7–8, 14
Kipling, John, 7–8
Kipling, Josephine, 7–8
Lahore, Pakistan, 5
Letting in the Jungle, 32
Loos, Battle of, 7
Mandalay, 5, 28–29
Meter, 5
Monkey People, 34
Morris, William, 6
Mowgli's Brothers, 33
Music-hall ballads, 5
Nationalism, 7
Natural Theology, 44–45
Neighbours, 23
Nobel Prize for literature, 4
Poe, Edgar Allen, 6
Poets' Corner, 8

Prophets at Home, 7, 22
Recessional, 8, 46
Road-Song of the *Bandar-Log,* 34
Roosevelt, Teddy, 7
"Scribbler, The," 6
Seal, white, 10–11
Second Jungle Book, 6
Seven Years' Hard, 6
Something of Myself, 5
Song in Storm, A, 7, 40–41
South Africa, 46
Stalky & Co., 6
Sussex, 30
Tennyson, Alfred Lord, 6
Thorkild's Song, 6, 30–31, 36
Thousandth Man, The, 5, 19
To Thomas Atkins, 27
Topsy, Deputy Uncle, 6
United Services College, Westward Ho!, 6
United States, 7
Vikings, 30, 36
War, weapons of, 42
Way through the Woods, The, 4–5, 38
Westminster Abbey, 8
White Man's Burden, 7
White Seal, The, 10–11
World War I, 7, 40